Readers Digest Very Little

READERS
Digest Very Little

or

A TREASURY OF
the
World's Greatest Litter

by IRVING D. TRESSLER

HOWELL, SOSKIN, PUBLISHERS

Manufactured entirely in the United States

OTHER BOOKS BY

Irving D. Tressler

The Human Body, How To Dispose of It

Early American Craftsmen and Crafty Early Americans

This book is dedicated to all those who won't try to read it at one sitting.

ACKNOWLEDGMENT

For permission to write certain portions of this text the author is grateful to the family living in the apartment beneath him, the members of which generously declined to play their flute, piano, harp, and radio between 2 A.M. and 7 A.M.

THE CONTENTS

The Contents

Readers Digest Very Little

The Blight That Flailed

EVERY second Thursday morning at 9 A.M. Henry Blight, a vacant smile on his round face, old shawl on the back of his head, pushes through the front door of the Teasdale, Missouri *Collect-Telegram*, barks out a verse of scripture in his thin, reedy voice, pushes his way past the desks of the editorial room, takes a short nap, and instantly starts dictating editorials. The editorials may be some fatherly advice to the U. S. Supreme Court about an important decision, a suggestion to ex-King Carol that he abandon Magda, or a polite note of warning to the Emperor of Japan to keep Japanese fishermen away from the Missouri State Fish Hatchery grounds.

By 10 A.M. Blight has four, maybe five, maybe

six or seven editorials finished. Then he sits back in his chair, unwrapping a book or two, glancing at a summons or two, or just staring stupidly until one or two. A little weary, a little constipated now at 93, but with something elfish in his expression, he is still the same old fool he has been and always will be in the hearts of Teasdale citizens. The walls of his office bear testimonials to the parts he has played in our nation's history—a wisdom tooth hanging from a golden cord and the words "From your friend John L. Sullivan"; a framed photograph of Harding, with "—thanks from the one who lost his shirt to the one who won!"; a mounted telegram signed "Bob" and referring to an editorial campaign Blight conducted to persuade the late Robert M. LaFollette to get an eyebrow-trim.

The telephone gives a short, sharp bark—in Teasdale they do things differently—and it's a call from the Dalai Lama. The door opens and in comes the press room manager to discuss a new kind of ink the presses are using. Then a woman who hasn't slept for months comes in and wants suggestions on what she should read next. Next, a big horsefly zooms in through the window. Henry's office is open to the whole town, the whole world.

Henry Blight unquestionably is the leading figure of his community. How he attained that leadership and held it for more than 75 years is a story that reveals the secret of all leadership.

As a very young man, politics was an essential part of Henry Blight's daily existence. He chuckles fondly now, and you sit in a delighted doze as he tells how he used to bribe the family dog to take his castor oil for him. "But it wasn't so funny," he adds soberly, "when the coat hanger broke and left me stranded there on top of that mountain. If I hadn't had my tonsils out long before I would never have heard Lillian Russell, and you may quote me on that!" His thoughts wander a little these days, but the mind of Henry Blight is as clear and direct as it ever was.

The *Collect-Telegram*, when Henry bought it, had a paid circulation of 42 copies. Today it has 47, including two paid subscriptions for the Blight family in Teasdale. That means that more than the entire population of the town take the *Telegram*.

How many other small-town newspapers can show a like coverage?

When Blight took over the *Telegram* it had a weekly payroll of $75 and more than once the staff had to wait for its money while its editor paid for a cable of advice to the British Prime Minister or some other foreign political leader. Today there's a payroll of $79.80 and "most of my employees have newer toothbrushes than I have," says Henry, "But I'm glad of it."

There's an intimate, friendly, family-like feeling about the *Telegram* shop. Ira Ponceforte started delivering papers when he was 8 years old and he's still delivering. A little flatfooted now at 76, Ira manages to support a racing stable and two wives very comfortably on his modest salary, and when Blight is out of town he writes the editorials and empties the wastebaskets.

Emily Macklin is another. For seven weeks Emily worked as a bareback rider in a circus. One day Henry Blight saw her and persuaded her to take a course in riveting. She's been the business manager of the *Telegram* for 48 years, now, and cooks the best doughnuts you ever tasted. "I like my work," she says quietly. "It isn't like bareback riding, it's more porous, and there's a piggy-wiggy in every pot, aren't you?" At 84 Emily Macklin's mind is as clear as it ever was.

You have to work on the *Collect-Telegram* staff 40 years before you earn the little pink ribbon which marks you as a loyal staff member and removes you from the newcomer class. Blight then gives you a warm handshake as a bonus and puts up your name on a card with a gold star on it. When you work there 60 years you get another gold star. Only five people have three gold stars and a perfect attendance record for 75 years and they are allowed to go pretty nearly any place they want in the building. Blight says the war has boosted the cost of gold stars these days, but when you catch that little twinkle behind the serious blue of his eyes you know he'd rather sacrifice his eclair desserts for a week than deprive his co-workers of their hard-earned gold stars.

The *Telegram* is Henry Blight and Henry Blight is the *Telegram*, though they have never spoken to each other. The editorials of those 75 years show a swing from smug conservatism to liberal fanaticism and back to republicanism, with traces of Cubism and schism. Blight once wrote William Jennings Bryan that it was dangerous to abandon your overcoat too early in the Spring. Bryan never replied, and Blight has always treasured his carbon of that letter. He has nothing but contempt for the middle-of-the-roader. "You can't set a course and expect to steer both ways," he snorts. "An old dog isn't a young one, you know."

Blight was only 23 when he published his famous editorial, "*Where Are We Drifting, Missouri?*" It stunned Missourians, who were used to drifting every which way, but it brought about a clean-up of vacant lots all over the state, and the next month Henry Blight was asked to speak before the Teasdale Women's Sewing Circle. "It was the toughest decision I ever had to make," Henry tells you today, his blue eyes snapping, his mind wandering aimlessly around the room, peering into this corner and that. "I paced the floor all night, but at dawn I sat down and wrote a note of thanks, declining the honor. Then I posted it and went to bed and slept for 43 hours. When I awoke I heard a low rumbling outside, growing louder each minute. I walked out on the front porch and looked up the street. There, four abreast, came marching a parade of women bearing signs and umbrellas. They were headed for me, so I stood and waited. I knew I hadn't a chance, but I knew I was right, and when they finally stopped in front of me there was a sudden silence. "Did you ladies wish to see someone?" I asked coolly, my hands trembling so I could scarcely bite my nails. You never saw a more flabbergasted lot of women in your life. They just looked at one another. They had expected me to run like a beaten cur, and they had no answer to my deliberate stand.

" 'Shall we kneel and sing Oh, Susannah?' I asked. They knelt with me and sang, and they've been my friends ever since. But," and Henry Blight shakes his grizzled old mane reminiscently, "I wouldn't care to go through *that* again!"

Henry Blight is just plain Teasdale, just plain home town boy. Once each year for over 63 years citizens of Teasdale have gathered in front of his house and ridden him out of town on a hand-hewn rail. It never seems to affect him. Henry Blight is "folks" as they say out in Hollywood. He gets up at 6 A.M. each morning just as he did 50 years ago.

"I'm not so young as I once was," he says, his faded old mind wandering reminiscently. "But I'm nobody's pillow yet! Feel that!" He bares his muscle and asks you to feel the stringy old cords. "I can still pick up a hot waffle soaked in butter and maple syrup!" he chuckles.

Henry Blight will never be old. He's just folks, and folks is— Thank you, a cup of tea would be delicious!

Intimate Glimpses

IT HAS been related that a brash young reporter once approached Horace Greeley in his office and said he wanted a job. "All right, young man," Mr. Greeley failed to reply, "can you write a news story that will hold the readers in their seats?" The young reporter should have replied, "Mr. Greeley, you don't want stories that hold readers in their seats, you want stories that will knock them out of them —the kind that I write!" Unfortunately, the young reporter only said, "Yes, sir!" and Mr. Greeley did not answer, "Then I don't want you on my paper!" so this never made the anecdote it should have.

At the end of a long, tiring day in her laboratory, Professor Ernestine Michaelson, the noted physicist, was returning home when a strange man stepped out of the darkness of a doorway. The man got away, however, and Dr. Michaelson felt more tired than ever.

A ricksha runner in Tokyo once asked Admiral Moorsey how fast he wished to go. "Oh, fast enough to get me there," Moorsey replied. "That's fast enough for me, Admiral," answered the ricksha runner, and was off like a shot. The shot, however, fell short and Admiral Moorsey never reached his destination.

Dr. Theodore Sibley, the famous missionary-explorer, was shaving himself on the back of a water-logged crocodile one day when a native chieftain approached him and said, "Ain't the shaving light something awful here in darkest Africa?" Dr. Sibley realized the native only wanted a new blade, so he calmly drew one from his kit and handed it to the chieftain who immediately burst into a yell of gratitude and cut his throat.

It has never been told that when Napoleon was returning from Moscow, cold, hungry, discouraged, one of his officers cantered up alongside of him during the daily blizzard and laughed, "Well, boss, it looks as though it might snow again today, doesn't it?" Napoleon turned slowly around in his saddle and looked at the man. "I wish," he replied, "I wish—" and then fell into a profound doze, a thing which would never have happened had he been making the journey in one of the big, new, warm, air-conditioned cars such as we have on most of our railroads today.

Where Do Our Birdies Go and Where Do They Come From?

EACH spring and each fall, across the face of the world, following set courses of their own, birds fly in semi-annual migrations. Some make these journeys for the sake of food, some for the sake of propagation, and others because they feel they would scream if they didn't do something.

The migration of birds is one of the oldest phenomena and one which has always been fascinating to man. He studies their unmarked routes by fastening tiny metal bands to their legs and letting the little feathered bastards go where they please. In this manner an accurate record of the exact wanderings of birds is kept. Bird bands have been found as far north as the Arctic circle, as have cigarette butts

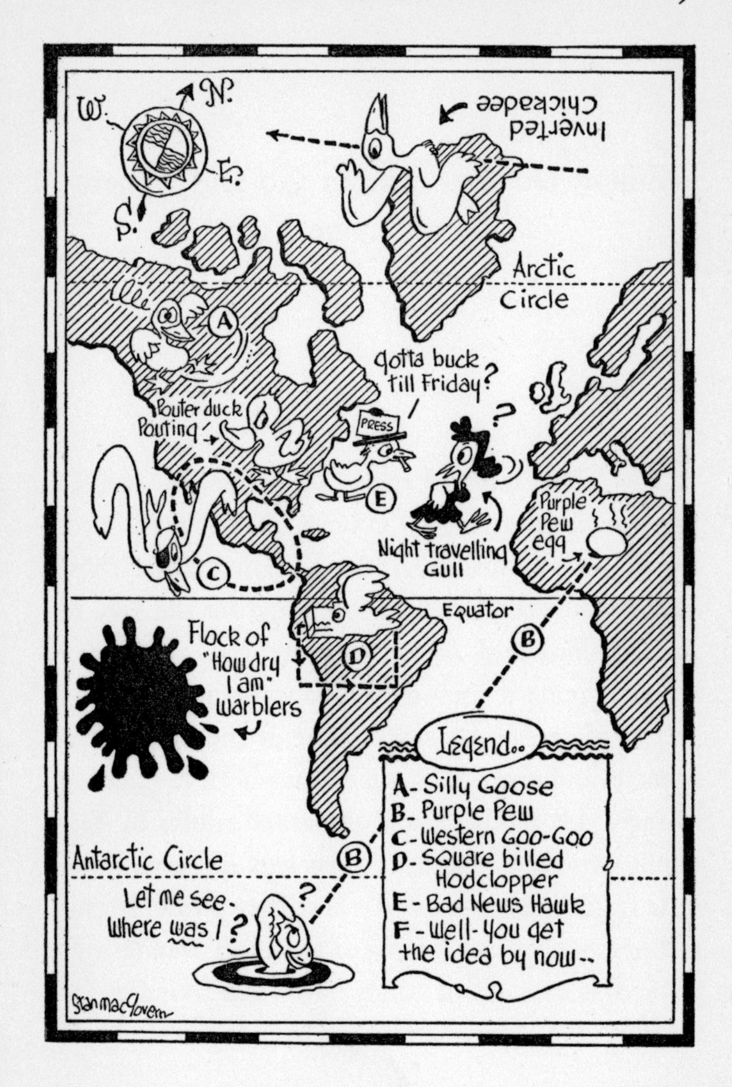

W.
N.
E.
S.
Inverted Chickadee
Arctic Circle
A
gotta buck till Friday?
Pouter duck Pouting
PRESS
E
?
Night travelling Gull
Purple Pew egg
C
Equator
Flock of "How dry I am" warblers
D
B
Legend..
A- Silly Goose
B- Purple Pew
C- Western Goo-Goo
D- Square billed Hodclopper
E- Bad News Hawk
F- Well- You get the idea by now--
Antarctic Circle
B
Let me see. Where was I?
?
Stan MacGovern

and bobby pins. The study of bird migrations has not continued long enough for man to say definitely that he can answer all questions concerning the mysteries of bird flights, but we have learned quite a bit about them and the birds which perform them.

Canada boasts an unusual fowl in the Silly Goose. (See map.) These creatures always fly in a great circle. Starting in the early spring, they set off with the perfectly good intention of flying somewhere, but early in their flight they lose interest and get panicky at the thought of going all that distance from home. In addition, the leader of each flock develops very cold feet and remembers he forgot to turn out the hall light, so eventually the silly geese make a wide circle and swing back to the place they started from, with everyone happy and no difficulties about border crossings to worry about.

The Purple Pew lives in Africa. This creature, half lizard and half fowl, is considered a great delicacy by the natives. Unable to lift itself more than three or four feet above the ground, it normally flies at a beat of 12 to the minute. It makes a single migration to the Antarctic each fall, but gets almost there, forgets where it's going, so backtracks to Africa where it builds a crude nest of twigs and old newspapers and lays as many as 43 eggs at one grunt.

The Western Goo-Goo is one of our native birds. It sets out in the fall and flies down the Pacific coast along Mexico to Panama where it goes through the Canal, goes across the Caribbean and Gulf of Mexico, then back up through Texas and to the western states where it started. Prior to the construction of the Panama Canal, the Goo-Goo was forced to go around Cape Horn, and regularly arrived back in the U. S. hot, tired, and out of sorts.

The Square-Billed Hodclopper is not a graceful bird, but South America has no need to be ashamed of this fowl. It was not its fault that Mother Nature built it on right-angled lines, so that it flies only in a great rectangle. The Hodclopper takes off faster than an old maid sighting a garter snake.

Birds travel either alone or with other birds, and their speed of flight varies widely. Some of the smaller birds fly faster than their own shadows, but very few can cover more than a continent or two each twenty-four hours. Fastest of the North American birds is the Bad News Hawk.

Migrations are just a matter of a sudden thought striking a flock of birds simultaneously, with all of them acting upon the idea at once. Most birds think it over very carefully for several months, corresponding back and forth, trying to find out what everyone else is going to wear and what route they are taking. The How-Dry-I-Am Warbler will not budge a flap unless it knows in advance what weather to expect, the condition of the rest rooms en route, and the names of three or four good places to eat. Then it sets out in enormous flocks of fifty to sixty thousand, which darken the sky, causing the warblers to alight and spend what they think is the night, the result being that they never get more than a few hundred yards from home.

The Night Traveling Gull, so accurate it can hit a hat at 22,000 feet, and has been known to strike a conductor's baton at an outdoor music festival, flies the last half of its 28-foot migration in a semi-daze. This bird, which merely shifts from one side of its nest to the other with the approach of spring and fall, is so lazy it uses only one wing at a time, which means that its flying is restricted to flopping about in vague circles and being very active in labor movements.

The Pouter Duck is relatively slow for its size and weight. A band fastened on a Pouter Duck in Montreal was found six weeks later, two feet away, with the duck pouting for all it was worth. The duck, when interviewed, guessed it would get where it was going, sooner or later, and immediately went into another severe pout, thrusting out its lower bill until it tripped over it.

Not all flying is north and south, no sirree bob! The Inverted Chickadee always flies east and west and upside down, the latter because it is so shy it cannot bear to have people on the ground stare at its under-carriage. As a result, its ceiling is the ground and when it tries to alight it sees stars.

From information possessed to date, the American longevity record is held by a Gold-Voiced Tenorbird which was caught at a women's club lecture in 1902. This bird, after recovering from the lecture, was released with a band fastened to its instep, only to be caught again in 1939 at another women's club lecture, mad as the dickens. It didn't mind being caught at a lecture again, but to listen to the very same lecture it had heard 37 years before was too much. It created a temporary stir by drowning itself in the pitcher of ice water on the speaker's stand.

Banding is aided by men and women in all walks of life. All over the world housewives bending over their tubs, politicians bending over theirs, catch birds and murmur "Izzums peshus sing dess fwightened to peeses?" as they examine the band on the bird and fasten a new one in its place. Then the bird, vomiting freely, is released and the bander reports the number to Washington.

If you see a bird, catch him and tie a band to his instep. If he has a band already, take down the number.

Advice to birds: if you see a human with a band in his hand, fly like the devil—no, fly like a Spitfire, it's faster!

Common to modern humanity
Is theater chair-arm vanity;
You never know quite
If it's left or right,
So you sit there in squashed insanity.

The House of Today

IN AN age of confusion it is a pleasure to present plans for the first house designed especially for it and its inhabitants: The House of Today. Here is a home for the typical American family of the 1940's, that closely-knit little social group which hasn't the slightest idea where it will be a year from now, and is perfectly willing to make a down-payment on anything. In the design of this house, tradition has been thrown to a friendly wind and the structure utilizes only materials native to its locality: orange crates, ticket stubs, silk smoking jackets, etc. In the average community this home can be erected and destroyed for less than the cost of prosecution of a good assault and battery case.

Modeled after political ideals, the building is not

quite square and is divided into rooms none of which are equal. The centrally-located bathroom has doors of 10-inch steel and is built to withstand sieges from all four sides for as long as a week at a time. In case of war, it can be quickly converted into a map room for the general of the defending forces.

There is no living-room because of the lack of time for genuine living in this era. The substitute is the Maze Room.

The house is erected on vaguely-placed stilts, permitting the structure to sway pleasantly back and forth in the breeze. Swinging doors are used everywhere except where really needed. There is no roof, which takes care of the ventilation problem and, in addition, allows us a look into the place. Where privacy is desired a gay beach umbrella is both inexpensive and a nuisance.

There are four separate entrances to The House of Today, but the conventional staircase-and-door entrance has been eliminated. Entrance is by means of a knotted rope suspended from a jutting beam; exit is by way of a 20-foot jump. This unique

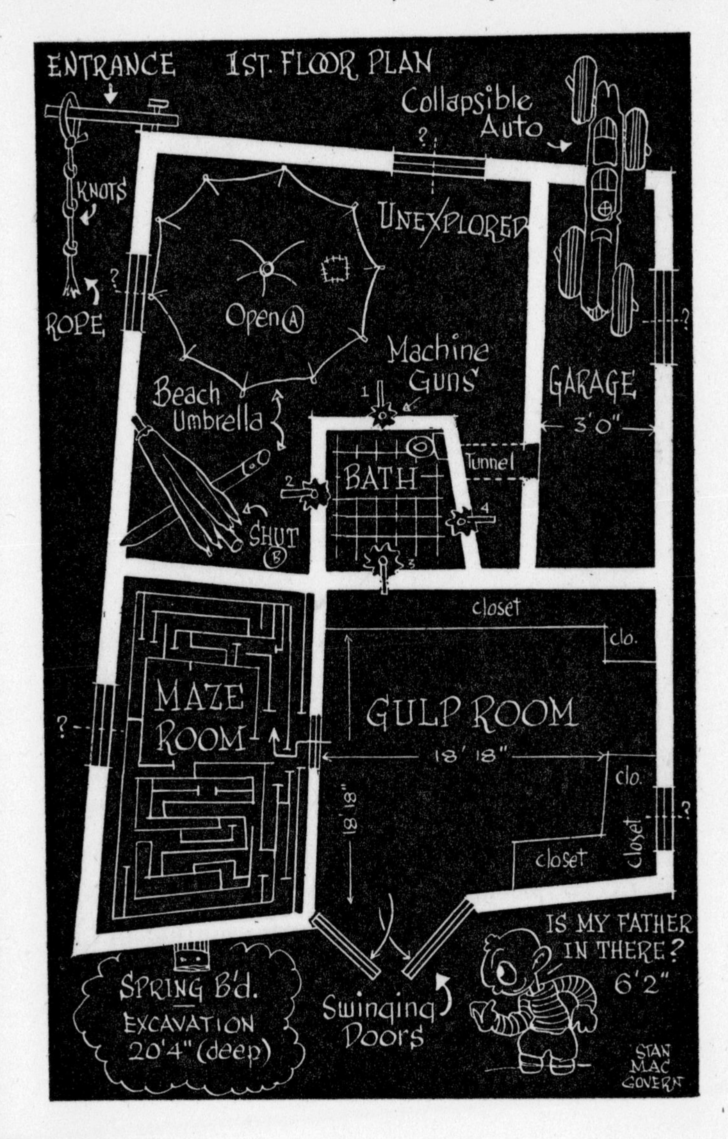
ENTRANCE
1ST. FLOOR PLAN
Collapsible Auto
KNOTS
ROPE
UNEXPLORED
Open (A)
Machine Guns
Beach Umbrella
SHUT (B)
BATH
Tunnel
GARAGE
3'0"
closet
clo.
MAZE ROOM
GULP ROOM
18' 18"
18' 18"
clo.
closet
closet
SPRING B'd.
EXCAVATION
20'4" (deep)
Swinging Doors
IS MY FATHER IN THERE?
6'2"
STAN MAC GOVERN

entrance-exit solution keeps out all but the dearest of friends and saves considerable expense in the form of foot-scrapers, door mats, etc.

The heating problem is answered by wearing warm underclothing in winter plus a consistently maintained visiting schedule with friends.

All rooms are on the same floor except the attic, which is in the basement, which is in the attic.

The dining-room is replaced by a Gulp Room.

There is no kitchen; each room has a wire connection with the nearest drug store fountain-bar.

The single-car garage, located underneath the house, is one-foot narrower than the average car of today, but that is not our fault. We were only trying to help out the Defense Program by saving blueprint paper. Rakes, lawn mowers, and other lawn and garden implements are suspended from the ceiling, permitting the driver to run directly into them without being forced to steer from one side of the garage to the other, as in the old-fashioned home. Exit and entrance to the garage are by way of a slight depression in the concrete beneath the transmission and rear axle, which is not so handy, but that's not our fault either, if you want to get huffy about it.

That is The House of Today: a confused structure for confused people in a confusing age.

Why Not Learn to Figure Skate?
or
Why Not?

WHY don't *you* take up figure skating? Make yourself into one of those jointless persons who skitter around an ice rink like a grasshopper on a dish of jelly. Buy yourself a costume and a pair of figure skates—it's easy once you get the knick-knacks of it!

The style and color of the costume are up to you. Corduroy wears the best in the seat.

Figure skates are different from ordinary skates: they have nasty little teeth on the front ends of the runners, to help you make jumps and tail-spins.

Figure skates are always attached to high shoes, which includes both the price and style. Each shoe is 15 laceholes high, so if you plan to go skating at 2 P.M. you start putting on your skates just after you discover the alarm clock didn't go off. Beginners sometimes use this lacing-up business as an excuse to stall off the moment when they'll have to stagger out on the ice for their first lesson. That's foolish. It's like pulling the sheet over your head when you hear a mosquito whining around your bedroom—sooner or later you know you'll have to come out.

Don't ask who originated this idea of breaking your neck on frozen water. Archaeologists have dug up samples of bone skates used 1,000 years ago by the Norsemen, but the first real mention of it in history was in 1396. It was on that date that a certain St. Liedwi of Scheidam, Holland, tried skating for the first time and took such a spill that she gave it up altogether and devoted the rest of her life to religious exercises.

Pepys describes the short petticoats of the Princess of Orange as she "did slide upon her scates, first upon one foot and then upon the other," but we'll bet it was petticoats and not "scates" that Pepys was most interested in.

In 1864 an American named Jackson Haines went abroad and "electrified all Europe" with his figure skating. Sixty years later a Norwegian named Sonja came over here and electrified the U. S. with hers, so we're even.

There's no mystery to figure skating. It's just the dreariest of the chilly sports and the chilliest of the dreary, etc. There are two known types of skating instructors: the big, smiling, kindly type and the spare, serious, snapping type. Yours is the second.

He starts you off by showing you how to make a right-footed curve to the left and a right-footed curve to the right. Then he demonstrates the left-footed left curve and the left-footed right curve. "There!" he barks, "those are the elementary edges. Now, go and practice!"

Practice is the professional word for figure skating. If you thought those years as a child at the piano or violin were awful then you haven't yet shaken hands with Monotony!

After months of practice your instructor graciously consents to stand and watch while you cut what you think are almost perfect circles with each foot. "Well," he growls grudgingly, when you have finished, "you *have* made a *little* progress. It's time you learned something about form." Whereupon he glides out over your poor, wobbly little circles and turns around.

"Look, my young hippopotamus!" he snaps. "Remember to keep your head up, and don't let your eyes fall on the nice. Learn to hold your body straight—not bent over like a postman's. Throw back your shoulders, expand your chest, let your arms have free play, bend your elbows, and make your hands face down and in! And in the name of Sun Valley, learn to bend your skating leg at the knee and turn the other leg out with the toe pointing down and out! Now, go and don't darken my floor again until you have practiced form for six months!"

Practice, practice, practice! After six months you are still not allowed to attempt even a bashful little spin or jump. Next, you must learn the Fundamental School Figures. And what are the Fundamental School Figures? Oh, they merely include the 3's, the loops, the 8's, the brackets, the rockers, and the counters. By the time you have learned the Fundamental School Figures many years will have passed. Your original instructor will have died. You will have made enough 3's and 8's to equal the sum total of the U. S. wheat surplus, with enough left over to feed the farmers.

Figure skaters smile only for cameras. Life is a mighty serious thing to them, and there's too much to be learned during its short span to waste precious minutes on frivolities. The years slip past and the first thing they know there's gray at their temples and they haven't even mastered the Philadelphia Twist!

I have just ended 10 years of practicing inner edges and outer edges, with one conclusion: It's easier to keep your tongue away from a hole in your tooth than it is to learn figure skating.

However, don't let me discourage you from taking up this popular sport.

Happy landing!

When buying a suit, I always find,
I'm never able to make up my mind
Until
The pill
Tries his salesmen's art,
And says, "But sir, this year it's smart!"
Whereupon
I re-don
My sagging old garment
And walk away from the moustached varmint.

Statistics Show

Dear Subscriber to News Comment:

We know you won't mind if we make this an almost personal letter about yourself and your friends.

You see, News Comment is proud of its subscribers, so perhaps you will be interested to know some of the things our research department has discovered about you and your fellow readers:

Death, as it must to all men, may come to you this year: therefore, one of you has insured himself for $17,000,000, but hasn't paid the premium yet. Two of you are not kings of small Balkan monarchies. One of you has never dropped a 16-pound bowling ball on his boss's toe. Many of you are normal, alert Americans, earning less than $14,000 annually and retaining a lifelong desire to know how it would really feel to hit someone with a custard pie. Many of you still possess your original teeth, and your average age is quite high due to the modern vogue for living. Some 76% of you attended college, 47% graduated, 964 are college presidents, and 3,389 are general handymen.

Home lovers, many of you have married. Most of you have married an average of 3.2 times and have 12.7 children. Each one of you has had every part of his body except the heart removed at least once in major operations, and you men readers shave on an average of 4.1 times per week. Everyone of you women uses five quarts of nail polish every nine years, and none of you know what a polyp is.

At home, all of you are busy from dawn to dark. 43% of you make a hobby out of telling women that their slips show. 17% have been arrested for dropping flower pots out of windows. 74% have never seen Ben Bernice in a pair of Jantzen swim trunks. All of you collect something, from famous safety pins to dog leashes owned by ex-senators. In brief, your lives are so full, so varied, so meaningless that 89% of you suffer an electrical discharge from each hair follicle following sustained periods of drought and no News Comment.

All told, you entertain 2,300,000 dinner guests each week-end and, all told, only 2,346 of these guests ever invite you to their houses for dinner in return. Most of you like to argue with your neighbor, and 97% of you let your neighbor win the argument because he is bigger than you are and once took lessons in jiu jitsu, even though News Comment keeps you so much better informed.

According to our very latest survey, the men among you are 67.2% better informed on art, religion and education than the average truck driver, and 99.6% of you know that the cowbird lays its eggs in smaller birds' nests and then walks away with a coarse whistle of satisfaction. The women among you are 93% uninformed and don't give a damn.

This is the News Comment community of which you are a member, but something dreadful is about to happen unless you help. . . .

Your subscription will expire in 3.5 years unless

you fill out the enclosed blank. We want you to stay on with us and share the many dividends we hope to promise; therefore, we are offering you a special Old Friends Are the Best subscription at the unheard-of rate of seven years for $10.00 or what have you.

These rates are open only to old subscribers like yourself and to those who can't resist a bargain. Enclosed with this letter is a carrier pigeon. The pigeon may be somewhat squashed, but please fill out the Old Friends Are the Best Special Subscription blank attached to the pigeon's leg, and toss him out of the nearest window. If we have not received your renewal order as a member of our Community of Intelligent Medium Intelligences within three months then we shall conclude the pigeon was incapable of sustained flight.

We know you want to maintain the ancient friendship that has existed between us.

Cordially,

The Circulation Department

Some day they'll build an airplane
So super-super fast,
When a plane, and a rumor start even,
The rumor will come in last!

Me and My Birds

IT WAS a warm, sunny morning as I sat reading my newspaper on the tiny brick terrace which my wife and I have grown to love so desperately. Not everyone in New York City can read his newspaper on his own brick terrace I was telling myself, and myself was just about to reply that not everyone wanted to, when suddenly a bird swooped down and alighted in front of me.

His tail was a greenish-red and fully 40 inches long, and about his eyes were pale yellow circles; his breast was quite bare of feathers, and his back had that soft smoothness of an old coat elbow.

"Chirr-up, chirr-up!" he sang, then paused and cocked an eye at me.

"Oh-lee-oh-lay-ee-hoo!" I replied, and he jumped a foot.

"Chirr-up?" he queried again, cocking his head and backing away.

We got along famously after that, the Bare-Breasted Whoo-ee and I. He stayed in our garden the entire summer, seeming to prefer to remain among the petunias and begonias and catawbas, although I tried several times to tempt him with Sal Hepatica. We had other bird visitors that summer; in particular I remember three thrushes: a Wood Thrush, a Hermit Thrush, and a Pointed Thrush which I made myself.

I found the Pointed Thrush most friendly. It has a long tail and a bill with a curve something like Bob Feller's. Its call note resembles a dentist's drill. Song is lacking, thank God. Its habits are solitary, moody, silent, depressing, mournful distressing, obnoxious, dolorific, irritating, offensive, revolting, loathsome, execrable, odious and tiresome. Many people do not care for the Pointed Thrush.

We have many sparrows in our little yard; a greedy bird and quite inept in the processes of working for an honest living. I have seen a sparrow pulp down an entire rose leaf merely to obtain the few tiny aphid on it, instead of daintily picking them off one by one. Yet they are extremely friendly birds. They are members of the European Skylark family, which migrated to this country about the same time as the Boston Tea Party, which did some skylarking of its own. Since earliest times sparrows have followed the horses.

Often we have a number of Purple-Throated Wobblers as guests in our garden. About half of the members of the wobbler family are gifted songsters; the other half think they are. They prefer insect food on the wing, but will accept it on a platter. Their wings are long and powerful, but they are inclined to press their approach shots. When resting at night they sleep lengthwise on their perches, asking no quarter and very seldom getting one. They have been found as far as 4,000 miles at sea, which from our brick terrace would place them somewhere near Paris, as the wobbler flies. Their love song consists of a prolonged snort followed by an embarrassed clearing of the throat and a foolish giggle. They are ideal house pets and can be trained to catch flies and mend old stockings.

For a week last winter we had with us as a guest a Red-Eyed Weeper. He came down on our terrace as it was getting dusk one January day, made a forced landing at about 60 miles per hour, then turned around and taxied back up to our terrace furniture. He was a handsome bird. His plumage consisted of a brilliant green breast slashed with scarlet stripes, while his back boasted an all-over pattern of blue dots on a background of yellow. His feet were completely flat and he walked with a pained expression. Also, he lithped when he thpoke.

The way this weeper ignored my wife and me was anything but flattering. He seemed completely uninterested in good books, art, or any of the better philosophies. Indeed, all he appeared interested in was food, which we gave him. Not until the night before he left did I manage to extract any information from him. Then he told me that the Red-Eyed Weeper was common to every country in the world. It builds its nest in low, marshy places and lays from two to twenty red-plaid eggs, the number varying with the humidity. It has an exceptionally powerful beak, so sharp and strong that it can easily drill holes in brick pavements and steel bank vault doors in its ceaseless search for grubs. As a result, it is disliked by superintendents of city paving projects and by bank presidents. New Englanders believe that when the Red-Eyed Weeper is heard drilling on a bank vault door it may rain the next day or again it may not.

You, too, can entertain your feathered friends in your home if you have a backyard and a tree and some bushes and shrubs and a bird bath and a fence and some grass and some patience. A little effort, a few crumbs—you will never know until you try it what fun, what true pleasure there is in caring for an exhausted Oh-Yeah or a passing Ulp.

Birds are grateful for this kindness and frequently repay you. Three years ago an exhausted Poop-Poop plopped into our yard. I fed it and gave it a bed and took care of it until it was strong enough to fly on again. Two years later I had a flat tire while going 75 m.p.h. on a Montana highway. The car started to swerve violently from one side of the road to the other and I lost control completely. My wife said good-bye and was about to open the door and jump when suddenly we heard the low poop-pooper-doo cry of a Poop-Poop. I looked out of the car window and there, flying right along beside my arm with a tiny card in its beak, was the Poop-

Poop which I had nursed back to health two years before. The card said on it: "Here's the control of your car. I happened to be flying past and saw you lose it." If we had not befriended that little Poop-Poop two years before we would not be alive today. To me, birds are my best friends.

Splatter

"HE WAS the sort of guest who uses a guest towel and then refolds it as though he hadn't."

Weeval Mettem

"She was quite upset by his blatitude."

Izzy Bright

"He suffered terribly from the bitter scold."

Justin Otter Sapp

"Parachute jumping in the Army is done from a height of 750 feet. If the chute fails to open, you make it in two seconds, flat."

Major U. B. Cairful

"All my best frenzies are women."

Grace S. Slender

"He was over 80—long past the age of discretion."

Judge Watts Dewing

"Many authors who expect their books to change the world fail to realize that it may be a short change."

Eddy Cantor Canny

Small Town Makes Good in a Big Way

FIVE years ago Boonhaven, Michigan, was bankrupt. Good Humor men were leaving by the cartful. The five-and-ten stores had ordered their hair-curler demonstrators to other cities. Locomotive engineers looked straight ahead as they rode through the town. And great stands of spruce stood dejectedly at the edge of the village alongside even greater and more dejected hamburger stands.

Boonhaven was down and out and knew it.

Today Boonhaven, Michigan, averages 22 arrests for speeding per week. Mandolin and viola lessons picked up from almost nothing to 16 three times each week. Happy, busy citizens contentedly roll huge olive pits in their mouths all day long. And on clear winter nights it is possible to get Myrt and Marge from Buenos Aires.

All because of the simple foresight and faith of a storekeeper who got an idea and held onto it by the tail.

Five years ago Louis Glazer sat in the back of his magazine and stationery store in Boonhaven at closing time and tried to recall whether he had had two or three customers that day. None of them had bought anything; it hardly seemed worthwhile continuing the business which his father's father had started and been unable to stop. Louis Glazer started thinking. Every other business in Boonhaven was like his. What was needed, he reasoned, was more patronage.

Then he retired, exhausted, for the night.

Next morning Glazer was up bright and early, drank two cups of coffee for breakfast, suffered a slight pain in his right side, shook some ant powder about the door sill, and went downtown. On his way he stopped to see Allan Fortis, the hardware dealer, Charlie Moons, the banker, and Avery Slichter, the garage owner. To each he gave a cigar and presented his idea. They liked both.

Louis Glazer's idea was this: Boonhaven must become the center of something-or-other for the

United States. It didn't matter what just as long as it was the center and got publicity. Next, something that had always worried Louis Glazer and therefore must worry millions of people like him was the lifelong curiosity to know why elephants keep up that constant swaying back and forth as they stand. Boonhaven, sloe-eyed little Michigan town, must become the center of Elephant Sway Research for the entire United States and perhaps the world.

That night a gigantic mass-meeting was announced for the courthouse lawn. Practically the entire population of Boonhaven turned out and marched past to see Clark Gable in his latest picture at the movie house down the street.

Next day Boonhaven's population leaped in size when Louis Glazer borrowed the money from Charlie Moons' bank and bought two elephants from a bankrupt zoo. One of them was an African elephant and had ears larger than King George VI, and the other had arthritis very badly and hadn't swayed back and forth for years, but it was a start.

Glazer then persuaded Charlie Moons to lend the town money enough to purchase a copy of every book and pamphlet on elephants that had ever been published.

For two days each Boonhaven man was encouraged to contribute two hours of manual labor to help dig a gigantic elephant trap in the center of the main street. The womenfolk made doughnuts and coffee, and square dances were held in the strangest places. Then the vast pit was covered over with brush and DANGER signs were erected around it. In the very first hour 12 tourists' cars, which otherwise would have scurried throughout Boonhaven, were caught in the pit. The menfolk fell to with a will as each car tumbled into the pit, square dances were served, and doughnuts and coffee were held in the oddest places. The cars were quickly removed to the hospital and the tourists sold as junk, or maybe it was the other way around; it's so difficult to think straight these days.

Boonhaven, Mich., is no longer the discouraged town it was five years ago. Today it boasts the only Home for Retiring and Shy Elephants in the United States. Scholars come from all over the world to study and giggle in the stacks of the world's largest collection of elephantia in the

$100,000 James M. Humph Memorial Library. A $500,000 E.S.R.C. (Elephant Sway Research Clubs) building dominates the town and serves as the national offices and convention center for the annual gathering of the 10,000 delegates from the 13,000 E.S.R.C.'s located in every state and 16 foreign countries.

A school for teaching people how to ride comfortably and gracefully on elephants' heads has students come to take its six-week course from 32 states. Men who haven't had an elephant hook in their hands for years now toil happily in three shifts in the various industries which have sprung up (women are not allowed to toil in shifts, but may wear skirts and blouses if they wish): an elephant toenail polish plant employing 700 men and 83 elephants, a factory which manufactures 1,500 long-handled back brushes for elephants per day, a firm specializing in elephant howdahs with kitchenettes and bedrooms.

There are no mice in Boonhaven today. Knowing how elephants fear these tiny creatures, the Boonhaven Chamber of Commerce offers 25 cents a pelt reward. Most Boonhaven females eke out their family's income by catching mice, which are then put through a special process in the new $1,000,000 community canning factory, so that today Boonhaven Vegetable-Meat Soup is known the length and breadth of the country. As a result, the elephants are terribly happy and cheese sales have doubled and tripled.

No direct progress has been made in discovering why elephants insist upon swaying back and forth, but Boonhaven is thriving and famous and that's what really counts. And it's been frightfully good fun writing this and not once mentioning the Republican Party, or something about a trunk.

Come and see me as soon as you get settled. Promise?

How We Built a Swimming Pool for $3.02

By Mrs. Jeffery Busch, R.F.D. 3, Aspen, Pa.

IT WAS a pretty discouraging prospect we surveyed as we stood staring at the rambling old house and the horrible tangle of a yard surrounding it. My heart sank at the thought of trying to make something homey and attractive out of such a place as this. But we were in no position to ignore the will of my late uncle; this *had* to be our home and we had no choice. It was up to us to make something out of it.

My uncle had gained his living through the collection and re-sale of used metal objects (and a very nice living it was, too, in case you start any of that curled-lip stuff). Unfortunately, at the time of his death he was badly overstocked and the yard was a dreadful maze of old cars, stoves, necktie racks, and worn-out parking meters. What could anyone possibly do with such items? That was the challenge thrown to us. We determined to answer it and show the world that beauty is not where you find it, but where you make it.

For the next two years we had the time of our lives. The first thing we did was touch a match to the old house. How we cheered as it shot up in flames with only two fatalities and a small rash on the back of one fireman's neck. Then we obtained an FHA loan and, before the embers were hardly cool, commenced a $75,000 gatekeeper's lodge on the site. But there was still the yard. How could we ever do anything with such a hopeless plot?

Carefully we set about effecting the metamorphosis. We planted Sweet William, English ivy, and kohlrabi in all the tin cans and arranged them in concentric circles of old truck tires, with outshooting spurs of old Maxwell frames. The whole contrived to give the effect of a Japanese flag after a hard blow and, I believe, contributed much towards our eventual award of second place in the

Green County Better Gardens Contest. You can just bet we were pretty proud of our efforts!

But this was only a start. We still had 42 upright radiators, 17 water closets, 10 iceboxes, 6 sunray lamps, 53 coaster wagons, 7 furnaces, and a portable garage. How could we possibly utilize these in our crusade for beauty?

Grasping the garage firmly, we planted it squarely in the center of the yard. Then, in a flowing design radiating from the garage we set out the iceboxes, water closets, radiators, furnaces and coaster wagons in a series of tight little patterns, filling each item with soil and planting them alternately with petunias, begonias, and fuchsia. The once-drab junkyard became a veritable fairyland, and we had accomplished it all at a cost of only a few week-ends of happy toil.

We still lacked a swimming pool. After all, we had a shovel, and we were connected to the city water main, and we knew how to swim. Why not? At the start of the second year we decided to build the pool ourselves.

We agreed upon a reinforced concrete pool 20 x

40 ft. and 9 ft. deep at the deep end, though goodness knows where else it could be 9 ft. deep. It was to slope to 3 ft. at the shallow end, would have a scum gutter, and would be wired with an automatic red light to warn of dead muskrats and snapping turtles.

Early that spring we set to work. The excavation was simple. My husband happened to be working, at the time, for a powder company, so it was only a matter of a few nights to carry home enough dynamite to blast out the hole for our pool. As the excavation progressed our neighbors commenced to share our excitement, and many of them showed their confidence in our construction abilities by purchasing new swimming suits and canceling their vacation plans.

By May the hole was almost ready for the concrete, but we had discovered to our dismay that the soil was terribly loose and gravelly. Fearing cave-ins during the hardening of the cement, we papered the sides of the excavation with old copies of DUN'S REVIEW. The paper was held in place by slide fasteners which were sewed in during the course of an evening of games and popcorn-making to which all the neighbors were invited and asked to bring one slide fastener as the price of admission.

At last came the time to pour the cement and you can imagine how excited we were. One neighbor borrowed a portable mixer from a paving job up the street; another borrowed a load of sand; another found some bags of cement in a neat pile somewhere, and so it went. The proportion we settled upon was one part of cement, two parts of water, three of sand, and just a dash of rum. At first we got too much rum in the mixture and, as a result, the shallow end of the pool smells a bit strong even today. As each section of the pool was poured and zipped a happy cry went up from the weary workers, but by dawn we had a swimming pool, and all for a total cost of $3.02, the price of the rum.

We have added trimmings to our pool, of course, little touches such as an old plank for the toads to hide under and an ashtray on the diving board. Our chief problem has been the growth of algae and neighbors. The former we get rid of by scrubbing and using copper sulphate every five or six weeks.

The latter we try to discourage by frequently draining the pool.

Did we have fun? Well, I guess! We wouldn't trade our pool for anything. On long hot summer afternoons as I sit in the water on my inner tube, one toe hooked in the scum gutter, my eyes fill with tears of thankfulness for the simple sacrifices and friendly cooperation which have given us more fun than a barrel of monkeys, and at so low a cost! You don't have to be a movie star to own a swimming pool in your own backyard, that's what I'm ready to tell the world!

From My Own Treasury of the World's Greatest Letters

NOT so long ago there was published a book entitled "A Treasury of the World's Greatest Letters" and, if one can believe all one reads these days, it is a fine collection. I, for one, am more than willing to concede a First Class ranking to this book, and I haven't the slightest doubt that it will eventually make one of the more stirring movies of the Forties.

The weakness of Mr. M. Lincoln Schuster's collection, it seems to me, is that he has concentrated almost solely upon letters reflecting the great personalities, great events, and great ideas of history. In brief, you and I have been left out, since it is unlikely that we shall ever write any letter that will reflect a famous personality, event, or idea of our generation. It seems as though there should be some recognition of those notes and messages which the great mass of mankind has and always will write to himself and to others. *They* are the true reflections of an age and its inhabitants.

For example, here is a yellowed scrawl which I found inside of the third chapter of a copy of Morgan's "U. S. Constitution—The Rise and Fall of Nullification."

> *Darling—*
>
> You'll find some cold ham and milk in the icebox, and there's also some custard. Kitty asked me to go shopping with her and stay uptown for dinner and a movie. I won't be home too late.
>
> *Muzzy*

Just how this note chanced to get in a book on the U. S. Constitution is neither here nor there. Still more puzzling is how it happened to get as far as the third chapter or exactly two-and-three-quarter chapters past the last point I remember reaching when Ed Cruton called up and suggested that I come over and see the movies of his fishing trip. (I was torn between a desire to continue learning something about the Constitution, something I have always promised myself, and spending an evening with comments which started, "Now, this is a poor print, but—.")

The important point is not the particular letter, though I recall that there was *not* any custard in the icebox and I had already had a ham sandwich and a glass of milk for lunch, but the fact that it represents thousands of notes left behind by wives for husbands, down through the ages. It is, like the empty salt cellar and the dull carving knife, an intimate reflection of the home and man and all that both of them stand for, and do! It deserves a place in any real collection of the world's important letters.

Here is another note, which I found in the left pocket of my winter overcoat when I got it out of the moth protective bag for use last winter. It (the note) was badly wrinkled and at first I was about to throw it away as either some idle scribblings concerning the heiroglyphics on the tomb of the Theban dignitary, Per-neb, made during a visit to the Metropolitan Museum, or else it was a code known only to me and Washington, asking me to board the first train for the District of Columbia and informing me that a White House car would be waiting outside the men's washroom in the Union Station. I quickly discarded the latter possibility as absurd as I never use the washroom in the Union Station in Washington and the State Department knows it. Then I commenced to recognize the writings as some hastily taken-over-the-phone directions on how to reach a friend's home for a week-end dinner date.

The Note	*The Note Deciphered*
Tk FTr. to Wsh4 ch to AA—off 168 nt Bldwl—4 bl n lft on Hlsy Ap. 8a—	Take F train on subway to Washington Square-4th Street Station and change to AA train. Get off at 168th St. but don't get off at Baldwell Square. Walk 4 blocks north and turn left on Hilsey St. and the apartment is 8A.

That, to me, is a perfect example of a minor brick in the structure of our civilization, but it is these same small bricks which *in toto* constitute the mammoth dwelling which is our society. Well, anyway, it would be in *my* book of really great letters.

Here is a letter that got stuck between the second and third drawers of my desk and probably would have stayed there until we were dispossessed if I hadn't tried to find a pencil one day.

Dear Anne and Irv:

Well, we finally reached home, "tired but happy," as they say in the old country. It was a wonderful trip and most of the pleasant memories we shall always have of it are due to the wonderful time we had with you. I can't begin to tell you all of the nice things we said to each other about you two on the way home. I guess they are best expressed in the words of Bill when he leaned over and said to me after we drove away from your place that morning, "You know, that was the nicest visit I've ever known." And that's really something when Bill says that!

Anyhow, let me in my small way thank you for a wonderful time with "two wonderful people"! And I hope if ever you come to Highland Park you'll promise to stay with us. Thanks once more.

Sincerely,

Celia

This is representative of the bread-and-butter letter, a form of thank-you note that has been written and received by mankind almost since time began. There are dozens of others that should go in this book of great and representative letters of our age, but I think you get the idea. Besides, my garters are slipping and I think I hear Mr. Schuster at the door.

Male or female feels half-stripped
If a zipper comes unzipped;
But there's still no perturbation
Of a like humiliation,
As to start to stuff your face
And have your host commence a Grace.

This World of Ours

How Many of These Facts, Which You Learned In Grammar School, Do You Remember Now?

HUMAN BEINGS learn rapidly, more rapidly than any other mammal. They also forget more rapidly. We spend eight years in primary schools, learning facts about the world we live in. How much of this information do we remember now?

Let us start with fire. This is not a substance, it is something happening, and may consist of one, two, three, four, or five alarms. Only the three, four, and five alarm fires are worth getting up in the night and putting your pants on to go watch. When a candle burns, the wax is consumed and heat and light are produced. If you place your hand over a candle flame, yells and oaths are produced.

Air is a cousin of fire by a second marriage. Air is what planes fly in and employers give their employees. If you put a mouse underneath a large glass jar it immediately grows very self-conscious. Air is very necessary in our lives because it lets us know when dinner is ready and gives some life to soda water and ginger ale.

How did our earth get here? Many, many years ago, before even Irene Rich was born, our earth did not exist. It is nonsense to go any further because it's just so much conjecture, although a first-rate conjecturer gets paid mighty, mighty well these days.

But we are neglecting geography. Let us take Canada, our neighbor. Canada is the third largest country in the world. Though larger than the U. S., she only knits one-tenth as many bright pink baby garments. There is more gold in Canada than in Ft. Knox and the teeth of Harlem combined. Canada is bounded on all sides. She has an Arctic air mail, but prospectors don't write many letters. They would rather receive them. The St. Lawrence river is Canada's mightiest; it drains a territory of 500,000 square miles, containing one-half the fresh water and most of the plaid flannel shirts in the world. If the St. Lawrence seaway project is realized it will drain most of the U. S. Treasury, too. On its 2,000-mile course the St. Lawrence takes one enormous leap at Niagara Falls, turns a lot of dynamos, thrills a few newlyweds, and finally rushes crazily into the sea.

Canada is not like the United States because it has immense silences, but Canadians and Americans are alike as two p's in poppy. The gap between Canadians and Englishmen is far wider than that between Canadians and any other people, especially when dancing. Canada is a big country.

Gravity is a force. If it were not for gravity we would throw a ball into the air and it would stay there and then a big crowd would collect and we would be minus a ball. When you stop to think, you sometimes wonder why we always fall down and never up because it would be awfully convenient on stairways to fall up. The answer is, gravity is like a magnet and any two things in the universe try to draw closer to each other. Sometimes this is called necking.

Wood is lighter than water and floats well. If

you could put a wooden ship in a glass of water it would float and you would probably be offered a movie contract and be famous the rest of your life. By floating we mean that the object is equal in weight to the amount of water it pushes away; if a ship were made of solid steel it would sink to the bottom because it is heavier than the water it pushes away. Ship builders don't like to have ships sink to the bottom when they are launched because everybody bursts out laughing. That is why they build steel ships with lots of air spaces in them, because air is lighter than water.

Electricity is made of tiny particles which are sold to us at a big profit by private companies through the use of electric appliances. We could make our own electricity if we wanted to, but then we couldn't get any credit to buy new appliances. Materials through which electricity cannot flow are called non-conductors. Rubber is a non-conductor, so is a fruit pudding, but most wires are covered with rubber and not fruit puddings.

In automobile engines there are cylinders. Each cylinder is like a crowded bar-room during Prohibition. Gasoline is the Law. When the Law is sprayed into the bar-room the policeman acts as a spark and everybody in the room tries to rush out at once. This raises the roof, which is attached to a lever, and the motion of the lever, which is attached to the wheels of the car, causes it to move. The same thing happens to the other bar-room (cylinders) and the process is repeated over and over again. Eventually a few arrests are made, but the car keeps moving forward.

A long time ago, Archimedes,
Discovered, when taking a bath,
That a body will lose as many pounds
As the stuff it displaces hath.

But the loss is mathematical,
As is made so very much clearer
When you step from the tub and start to rub,
And see yourself in the mirror!

Heavens On Earth

On a warm August night in 1939 a small, red-faced, shy little man in shorts and thick-rimmed glasses was sitting in the middle of an Indiana corn-field carefully looking through a telescope at some-thing in the star-filled heavens above him. Sud-denly he gasped, looked again, then bounced up and ran for his farmhouse and the telephone. Via long-distance telephone he managed to shout to the director of a well-known eastern observatory the location and size of a brand new comet. There was a long silence at the other end of the phone and then the director shouted back, "That ain't no comet—that's a Chicago-N. Y. night mail plane!" and hung up.

The shy little man was Ernest J. Callahan,

farmer, who has spent the last 10 years exploring the skies with his telescope and recording his observations. Since 1930 he has been the discoverer or co-discoverer of 18,000 fireflies and 1367 airplane wing lights. He has charted and sent to astronomers more observations than any other living farmer, and he has received more letters with ugly words in them from leading astronomers all over the world than anyone else alive. To him the heavens are life. To his wife they are obscenity obscenity.

The story of this amateur astronomer starts with one February evening in 1930 when he was stumbling home from a quilting bee and tripped over a 40-inch reflector telescope in the middle of the road. As he stood there staring at this strange instrument a slow chill crept over him and he wished to heaven he had worn his overcoat; then and there he sank to his knees and resolved to devote the remainder of his life to seeing what there was to see.

When Callahan commenced his studies he had only this crude little 40-inch reflector. The 100-incher at Mt. Wilson had not long been completed, and the 200-incher now being completed had scarcely been dreamed of. Each clear night Callahan lay on his back in his meadows from sunset to sunrise and caught some of the worst colds and sore throats you ever saw. But slowly he came to know and understand that something was going on in the heavens above him.

In 1935 Callahan had his first success. He managed to catch a night hawk asleep as it was drifting overhead, and was awarded the Oscar Nimfen Prize of $1.23 for The Outstanding Discovery of 1935. Within two more years he had obtained new piston rings for his car and a new hall rug. Then one day he received a letter asking him if he would keep an eye out for a white-striped, male, grey, Persian cat, lost or stolen in North Indianapolis, reward. For two years Ernest Callahan allowed his land to lie fallow while he pondered over what he should do. Then he made his decision: his telescope was calling. He went back to it that night.

For a year he combed the skies, but this had nothing to do with his difficulty in making a parting. Many astronomers have spent lifetimes searching the heavens and have found only a permanent squint. At midnight of the 14th month Callahan detected a point of blurred red light high in the southern sky. His heart skipped a beat, but he was not worried—it had done that before. He pushed away his telescope, with the aid of two men and a tractor. In an hour he would look again; meanwhile he would beat his wife and vary the monotony of her farm routine. If the red spot was still there when he looked again, then he would know it wasn't a stop light.

That 60-minute period was probably the longest period in Callahan's entire life, unless you wish to count his first dance when a freshman at high school. Finally, though, he looked through the telescope again. The red spot had moved! It was a brand new comet and it was ripping across the southern sky like a suit of red underwear caught in a typhoon. Callahan ran across the fields of cornstalks, to his house, to the telephone, to bed.

Since that night Callahan has been accredited with the discovery more and bigger comets than any man in his predicament. His greatest comet—The Callahan Daisy—is between 2,000 and 5,000,000 miles in diameter (astronomers are not absolutely certain) and raced through space closer to our earth than any heavenly body since Dorothy Lamour's.

For the Callahan Daisy, which won't be seen in this country again until there is a Republican majority in the House, Callahan was given the Travelling Toothbrush Award by the American Dental Association, an honor bestowed upon only the most distinguished cases of caries and gingivitis. His wife was chosen Typical American Farmwife Parrafin User For 1939 and given a brand new Malay kris.

When you pay a visit to Callahan he usually shows you photographs of his latest heavenly discovery, in this case the Skunk Comet of 1940, so called because the comet and the other occupant of the cornfield were discovered simultaneously. Callahan reached the end of the cornfield before the comet did.

About Your Dog

(Condensed from Nowhere)

MOST DOGS have highly developed powers of smell. When they get too highly developed, give the dog a bath.

When giving your pet a bath, make sure no one else is in the tub. If the master of the house is occupying the tub, go to work on the master and dry him right down to the skin. Never let him lie around in the tub. When it is all over, pin a soft, warm towel about him and look the other way.

Many dogs are troubled with eczema. The trouble normally starts with an itching at the tail and proceeds until the family can stand it no longer. When this occurs, the family should be lined up in

HEEL!
aren't we all?
Stan mac Govern

the living-room and lots drawn to see who gives Fido the bath.

See that your dog bites the right persons. Nothing can be more embarrassing than to have a dear friend come limping into your home without a leg, protesting at the inhospitable attitude of your dog.

Many people now take their dogs with them on vacation trips. Dogs make fine driving companions. After a long, tiring day on the road, few things offer as much variety as a good fight between your pet and a strange dog.

If your dog isn't eating heartily try to tempt his appetite with new dishes. Creamed codfish on patty shells with ice cream should tickle his palate, or canned sweet potatoes on fried eggs with mayonnaise covered with crisp lettuce may do still more radical things. See that he always cleans up his plate and sits quietly after a meal.

When out walking, a dog should always be taught to heel. There is no particular reason for this except that it gives you a definite feeling that there is at least one creature lower than yourself. Dogs can be easily taught to bring in the newspaper, answer the telephone, reject postage-due mail, and many other helpful tasks about the home. A dog should never be struck. Always wait until the lesson you are trying to teach him for that day is over, then give him a gentle pop on the bottom.

The Growing Waddle Problem

(By the author of "Waistlines I Have Known," "Let Us Swing but not Sway," etc.)

MOST WOMEN walk at some time or other during their lives, yet few of them know how they look when they walk. Research on this important subject is almost non-existant because of the extreme danger involved.

After World War I a small group of interested scientists at Princeton commenced an elaborate program of observation and constructive criticism in this field, and very satisfactory progress was being made. One month after the program got under way two of the leading scientists disappeared while on a week-end visit to New York City. They were discovered several months later, married, settled-down, wiping dishes in the kitchens of attractive suburban homes, totally uninterested in the program they had started at Princeton. A meeting of the remaining scientists was immediately called at Princeton and it was voted to discontinue the research and commence work on some problem in which personal risk was at a minimum. Since that unfortunate happening little or no research in the feminine strut field has been carried on.

Women walk in many different ways. One of the commenest types is the Lame Hippopotamus Sway. This is found among middle-aged females and is pretty well limited to those weighing 200 lbs. or more. It is especially successful in women under 5 feet 2 inches in height. In most cases the knee joints of the victim are almost completely atrophied and the victim is unable to stoop and pick up anything less than a 10-dollar bill.

Then, of course, there is the My-Feet-Are-Simply-Killing-Me Hobble, found so often among elderly chorus girls. The owner of this kind of walk uses short, jerky steps and in general acts as though she were tiptoeing barefoot on a gravel road. Her face is contorted into a series of wrinkles which smooth out automatically upon meeting an acquaintance.

The well-known Dog-On-A-Leash Shuffle has increased enormously in the past 10 years and is particularly common among young married women in large cities. It is a halting, aimless drag, usually starting in one direction only to stop and make an abrupt right-angle detour, halting again, etc. The face of the owner is generally bored and retains a far-away expression, as though a dog on a leash at a telephone pole were the last thing in the world of which she was aware.

The Jenny Wren Jig is normally confined to small, doll-like females who take short little steps accompanied by a staccato tapping of high heels, with shoulders and hips jiggling in rhythm to the step.

All of us know the Clump Thump Stride, which is commonly limited to girls who are tall and "generously proportioned." The owner is usually of the athletic type; her stride is normally equal to that of Man O' War's and is accompanied by arms that swing in at least a four-foot arc. The shoes worn are low, comfortable "boats" and in the execution of the stride each foot is laid down full length from heel to toe, the movement being repeated over and over again by opposite feet in alternate succession.

The Learning-How-to-Roller-Skate Stagger is not a commonly seen step, largely because it is generally executed late at night by wives in their thirties, who "haven't been anywhere in a dog's age." It is usually carried out following an alcoholic party somewhere and is found surrounded by tired husbands trying futilely to suppress the too-loud and too-shrill laughter and defeat the warmly approved feminine suggestions of the moment to "go places and do things" at two in the morning.

We are all familiar with that jointless thing known as the Fanny-Slouch Roll. It is found among all stratas and types of women, from streetwalkers to business executives, and resembles the gait of a discouraged camel. The owner's body is always completely relaxed and the step is slow and leisurely; hips are twice normal size, and the derriere rises and falls from side to side with each disjointed step. The possessor stands a good chance of being whistled at by men of a not too desirable type.

The American college girl has a walk all her own

and it might best be listed as the Here-I-Come-Boys Step. The owner walks with bosom thrust out, neatly dressed, hatless, with a sort of diluted stride. She is one-third intent upon getting to where she is going, and two-thirds conscious of everything in pants that passes.

You're Growing Younger

By Doan B. Sill, M.D.

(Prize-winner, scientist, author of "The Runny Nose—How to Stop It")

THE HUMAN body is a series of organs, greatest of which is the grind organ, or stomach. It is all right to have a grind organ and a monkey, but one should never monkey with his grind organ. The next most important organ is the electric organ for home use and sells for $1,500 or less. Organs and the brain are connected by a series of hormones which send hourly messages back and forth and have every eighth day off. The messages are carried by glands, which spring from an immense network of nerves and arteries known as the Gland Canyon.

Most of us possess health in some form or other. Statistics show that only 10% of all males are below par and 90% are way over par and always expect to be, except for an occasional birdie or hole-in-one.

We are apt to forget that a clean mind in a clean body has nothing to do with health. Our body is like a great second-hand Chevrolet—it needs gas to keep it going. Unless you are full of gas you are inclined to be energetic and full of new ideas and very annoying to others. The machine that is your body comes from a tiny egg, which immediately divides into two daughter cells, which divide into two more daughter cells, etc. If this process is not stopped quickly and some of the daughters married off then the entire body is apt to end up in a cell.

The sound body lives in a sort of contented stupor. Its owner neither knows nor cares what goes on inside of him. Health is essentially a personal thing and should not be brought up at the dinner table unless the host or hostess opens the subject with a gracious discussion of her own disturbances. Health cannot be bought. The customary method is for the physician or pharmacist to hold up the patient.

Most of us like to poison our systems with poisons, although scientists now believe they have found a better way to do it. Poisons may come from within, or they may enter without knocking and plant themselves in the center of your living-room without so much as an "if you please." In either case it is generally much simpler to abandon the body and start all over again with a new daughter egg cell, otherwise you may be required to give up smoking, desserts, coffee cocktails, and class reunions. Hypnotics are used by many today, but the average physician is strongly opposed to concerts of any sort.

Your body must and does learn to adapt itself to all kinds of changes. One day you will swill down the most excellent sorts of drinks; the next day you down the most excellent sorts of swill; yet your body takes it all with only an occasional growl and backfire. One week the temperature may be 102 in the shade and the next week it will be 30 degrees cooler inside the town's leading theater, yet your skin takes it with a pleased gurgle. One minute you may be quietly listening to a favorite radio program and the next moment you find it interrupted by a long discourse on the benefits of Glug-Glug Tomato Juice, yet your body accepts it with only a 50-point rise in blood pressure, a slight reddening of the nose, and a doubling of the pulse rate. The human body is a wonderful machine.

Few of us realize it, but we are fortunate in the climate we have in the United States. It is stimulating because snow alternates with rain, making a nice gooey slop which causes us to stay indoors and reduces the chances for colds almost as much as it boosts the sales of rubbers. In summer, heat alternates with humidity, and many pay $12 per day for a room with a wash bowl and pitcher in an old summer hotel with rocking chairs and spittoons on the porches. In many parts of the South the change in temperature is so slight that the population sits in the shade all day, junior chambers of commerce are unknown, and life is thoroughly delightful.

The chemicals required for building up sound tissues in our bodies are not best obtained by eating certain foods, but by writing to the leading chemical products manufacturers and asking for free samples. Enclosed postage is not ordinarily necessary, although many have found that they sleep better if it is included. Do not pay too much attention to the current vogue for vitamins in food unless you have a financial interest in the company producing the product containing the special vitamin. Vitamins are found everywhere, especially in magazine and newspaper advertisements. Examine your periodical carefully before eating it as it may be taking an editorial stand which your stomach will reject.

Our own health is everyone else's responsibility and sometimes that responsibility is not properly exercised. Few things are more disheartening than to have successfully survived a major operation only to be accosted on the street with the question, "Well, where have you been lately—on a vacation?"

We should watch our social and psychological development and protect ourselves from too much excitement. The changing of position of an ash tray by a new maid can cause a purple face and a loud explosion. Too much cinema can be just as bad as too little. A flat tire while hurrying to a dinner party can upset the digestive system almost as much as a flat tire for a partner at the dinner party.

Serves Four Generously

THE CHILDREN came in at dawn, and let me tell you there was no disappointment on their faces when they saw that big steaming bowl of Tikkle's Pudding wating for them," writes Joseph L. Flutsow of 1378 Harrington Avenue, Detroit, Michigan. Mr. Flutsow is a carpenter by trade and his hands frequently get rough and coarse, just as his language does when he hammers a finger.

"I can still see that ring of eager, expectant faces around me at the table," Mr. Flutsow continues. "Lacking in calcium, lacking in proteins, lacking in energy, lacking in intelligence, in fact, lacking in most everything that Tikkle's has.

"Mummy was served first and she commenced eating noisily. Then came Robbie's dish, followed by Bill's, and if I hadn't held onto mine it would have gotten up and followed, too. I served myself from the big hot pot of Tikkle's Meat Ball Pudding, and in no time at all, or thereabouts, we had all finished our plates and started on a second helping. Then came a third and a fourth.

"The neighbors came in after a few hours and helped us, but we couldn't seem to get to the bottom of that big generous portion of Tikkle's Pudding. After a few days none of us could eat another mouthful, so I gave the can to the porter in our apartment building and he worked on it for a week. He couldn't find the bottom either, so he finally gave the can to a friend who worked on it for 10 days and passed it onto another friend.

"The last I heard, that can of Tikkle's Meat Ball Pudding was in the suburbs of Cleveland attending a lecture on 'China's Real Enemy—Mildew.' I think," concludes Mr. Flutsow, stretching himself luxuriously in his drop-seat, self-help, training set with the patented fastener, "the Tikkle Company is really too generous!"

It's awfully hard to tell whether a toad has or hasn't got mumps.

Many a girl has had dreams,
In which both her stocking seams
Stayed perfectly straight
From early till late;
It's a shame to awake from such dreams!

We Married on a Shoestring

(By the author of "And Then The Breaks Came")

ARNOLD WALKED clear across New York City to marry me, also to save a nickel. I had been getting my high school diploma; he had just received his 21st honorary degree. Both of us suffered from trichinosis. Everyone told us we were crazy to get married, but neither of us was afraid. What was most important: we were in love.

We were married and Arnold soon found a job. I had always dreamed a foolish, childish dream of marrying a gallant knight who earned more than $8.35 per week; now, all that was gone. Where could we live on $8.35 per seven days? We knew it was cheap living in central China, but neither of us had ever been introduced to Henry Luce or his wife.

For three weeks we slept in the old Schwab mansion. We had no heat, the water was turned off, lights had been disconnected, but the furniture was solid and substantial and the address was good. What sleeping we did was done in a hammock lent us by the U. S. Navy. For a table we used the top of an old Ford that had been wrecked outside our windows. We didn't need silverware as both of us preferred tearing our food apart, and as for linen and a cheese grater, well, we just did without.

Then one night Arnold came home and announced he had been given a raise. His boss liked the way he carried his sandwich board; now he was to get $9.00 per week and blow an East Indian gourd horn to call attention to his sign. We just had to celebrate somehow. I dug up an armful of dandelion greens; for dessert we had a perfectly gorgeous sunset.

Two weeks later we had a water softener installed in a piano box, which a friend of Arnold's had given him, and we moved in. It wasn't a Stein-

Stan MacGovern

way box and it was located way down on the lower East Side in a slum district, but it was our home.

The very first day, after Arnold had gone to work and while I was puttering about, cleaning up the breakfast things and sawing windows now and then, there came a noise at the door. I opened it and in walked a mongrel dog; he had only stopped by to say hello and, after looking about our house a little while, he departed, leaving me with a warm, tender feeling. The same afternoon two kindly old drunks wandered in, then a runaway dray horse, and finally the policeman on the beat. Less than 24 hours in our new home and already we had been accepted as members of the neighborhood! What next?

For $3.00 we bought a secondhand bicycle and Arnold built a generator with a pair of spools and a toothbrush. At night one of us sat and pedaled the bicycle to generate light while the other read. We didn't have a telephone and there wasn't an unabridged dictionary for blocks around, but we didn't care. It was our home and we loved it.

We couldn't afford matches, so each afternoon I started rubbing two sticks together. By supper time I had a cozy little fire going and a heaping cupful of hot water for Arnold's bath. "But when do *you* ever take a bath?" all my friends asked. "That's a secret!" I smiled, waggling a finger at them, but eventually Arnold got curious, too.

Arnold and I have no patience with people who say young folks of today don't dare fall in love because they can't afford it. Say, you can't expect to sit down and wait for things to be handed you on a silver-plated platter. Living in an abandoned mansion or a piano box is not easy, but life is never easy for those who get the most out of it. True love can never be discouraged if you provide a home for it, we tell all our friends.

Ideas for the Home

How the Thrifty Modern Bride Can Make Use of Duplicate Wedding Presents

Don't throw away that extra, new vacuum cleaner! Turn it upside down. Set the handle in a block of soft cement. Let harden. Presto! A nice new reading lamp!

The bride who receives two new cornets as wedding presents is fortunate. They make most attractive candlesticks for that vacant mantel.

Did someone give you subscriptions to "Fortune" and "Esquire"? Save your copies. Stack evenly side-by-side. Take old bath mat and spread on top of stacks. Result: one new, badly-needed coffee table for that bare spot in front of the davenport.

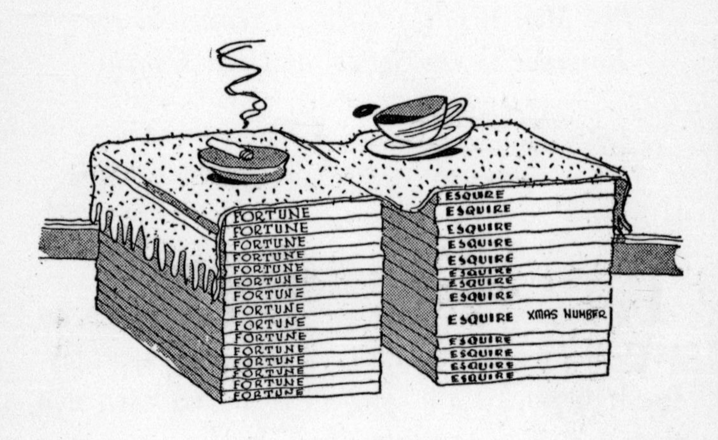

How Smart Are You?

By Professor Irving D. Tressler

The Man Who Installed a Doorbell at the Entrance to the School of Hard Knocks

THE LINCOLN penny is like an article on Why France Fell—we see at least one every day. But if anyone is still living in 3000 A.D., what will they deduce as to this civilization of 1941 if they suddenly uncover one of these little copper disks? If they still possess normal intelligence they should be able to make the following conclusions after a five minute study of the penny. (If they possess any intelligence they will spend it within the first two minutes!):

Evidently it was a small, low-value coin, which means that the civilization of 1941 possessed gum-vending and weighing machines. Such machines flourish best in railway stations, so a highly-developed transportation system must have existed, which means that there must have been thousands of grey-haired conductors about to retire after 50 years service with the same railroad during which their Tick-Tok watch never varied more than 15 seconds per year.

A surplus of wheat must have existed, otherwise these people couldn't have put so many stalks of it on their money.

The society was probably dominated by females; if it wasn't then the gentleman on the coin was a damn fool to wear that collar and tie.

The words *United* and *States* on the coin show that the government of this society was democratic in form, which tells that hotels, cigars, yachts, chorus girls, and liquor existed.

The words *In God We Trust* on the coin suggest a society of normal development, its members suspicious of each other and lacking faith in everything and everybody except a Supreme Being. (The low value of the coin also suggests the probable existence of religious groups with collection plate offerings.)

A complicated system of stocks and bonds must have existed because the coin is made of copper, and most copper is not mined without a friendly nod from such corporations as Anaconda and Kennecott, and these corporations aren't financed with hay.

There was city planning and definite forms of architecture because small coins of this type mean games of coin-pitching at sidewalk cracks, and sidewalks don't exist without buildings, and buildings call for (and usually get) streets. (Streets mean that there must have been parking difficulties, which means police tickets, which means a police force, which means an annual policeman's benefit ball, which means beer, etc.)

Many more deductions could be made from our Lincoln penny by the citizens of 3000 A.D. but, really, that's all I have time for now. A League of Women Voters representative is staring at me through the window, and I'm pretending not to be at home, and it's all terribly difficult, and I wish *I* were living in 3000 A.D.!

How I Escaped from Civilization

IN THE bar of a famous western resort hotel a tourist looked out of the window at the gorgeous display of snow-capped peaks, deep valleys, and saddle horses at $1.50 per hour. "This isn't the west I expected to find," he mourned, "I wanted to feel like Lewis and Clark, or De Soto, or maybe Chrysler. I guess you can't get to feel that way today!" Then he fell on his face and was carried to his room.

If this man had only known, adventure of the kind he sought was just at his elbow, or shinbone, maybe. The United States is honeycombed with wildernesses where no man has ever been seen with a Thermos bottle. Millions of square miles in extent, these untouched areas still offer the average person a chance to be just as uncomfortable as his forefathers were. Why not leave behind your bathroom scales and escape from civilization?

Last year, with 43 other people and 156 horses, I went on a pack trip. We left Biddeford, Maine at 10 o'clock one morning and by dusk were in eastern Idaho. For 10 days we didn't see a Defense poster or hear a soul ask how we are going to pay for all this. We didn't know whether Harry Hopkins was in his bathrobe or in London, and we didn't care. We saw three Frank Lloyd Wright houses, a flamingo's nest, and a bear's den, but no human habitations.

Weirdest of all sensations on this pack trip was our surcease from thinking. On the entire route we did absolutely none: all we had to do was worry. Under the greatest exhibition of stars since the Dempsey-Firpo fight we lay and worried about whether we had shut off the stove pilot, whether the telephone company had disconnected the phone as asked, and whether we had really put the silverware under the loose plank behind the baby carriage in the attic.

Twice we encountered the fresh spoor of station

wagons, those graceful, truly American creations that roam the estates of our land. We stopped for a day at a mountain-rimmed lake and caught huge trout, with little pats of butter on their backs and French fried potatoes. It was difficult to believe that less than 100 miles away lay gasoline stations with violet ray seats.

The average pack train makes less than three feet per hour, or about the same as a woman shopper with a blank check book. The newer, streamlined pack trains are much speedier and have an observation-club car on the rear. Here light drinks and sandwiches may be obtained, and gorgeous models sit in beautiful chromium armchairs soaking their feet in basins of cold water and dancing with shrewd, handsome-looking business men who always travel this smart, restful way.

On a pack trip you take what comes, no matter whether it is underdone and tough or just painfully sore. You wake in the middle of the night and find an ant-eater peering at you through your tent flap while behind him, each patiently waiting his curiosity-soaked turn, stands a line of weasels, water moccasins, vicunas, jackals, barnacles, and forest rangers. In the distance a mountain brook burbles swiftly past, on its way to join another brook and pour through fixed guide blades and eventually discharge itself in a direction parallel to the spindle of some great turbine in the latest world's largest dam. Far away the shrill cry of melting snow on gigantic peaks is heard. And from the top of a majestic pine tree a labor organizer peers and tries to estimate who and what he can organize.

One morning I sat on a rolled-up guide making notes as camp was being broken. The greenhouse had already been dismantled and, on the other side of me, the shooting gallery was coming down. Someone was shifting the buttons on an old mink coat, and scattered here and there over the rough ground were window screens, drunks, rubber boats, and pink, lacy underthings. Indians could have been on the other side of the mountain range, and buffalo might have been scratching themselves on the plains below us. But they weren't. (We could have been a Byrd expedition to the Antarctic, too, but we weren't.)

The cry of a lark and the lark of a good cry. The fun of waking to a cold drizzle. The horror of bathing in an icy pool with sharp, pointed rocks and gravelly soap for company. That is the wilderness of today. The best parts of it have already been photographed and sub-divided, but there are still choice sections left in South Chicago and East St. Louis. The good good earth clinging forever beneath your nails. The four-motored airliners groaning past overhead. Will I ever go on a pack trip again? *I* don't mind being asked, but won't someone please ask the horses?

Hints for the Woman Under Forty

(Condensed from Feminine Swank)

LITTLE TOUCHES like these really set your home apart from the everyday house: water for the finger bowls from a Kenya drinking hole; soap so hot that the servant screams as she brings it from the kitchen to the serving hall to the butler's pantry; a small, expertly-cut emerald at the bottom of each water glass; table linen woven in a 15th century sisterhood (before the Hearst agent arrived); favors and paper hats made from the original Versailles Treaty.

If you feel you cannot afford fresh flowers for your dining table in winter, have Tiffany's make up an attractive floral centrepiece of the more colorful precious stones.

You may wear last month's dinner dress with perfect aplomb. Simply cut the neckline low, fasten casually with the Kohinoor diamond or some similar stone.

A good panda fur is never cheap, but it is perennially smart, gives that air to any well-tailored costume. Send out a small expedition now: they are less expensive during the winter months.

An unborn-egret feather robe on your bed will outlast the most gorgeous of bedspreads and give you that delicious sensation of being different.

If you feel you cannot afford good maids *and* good food, do without the food.

A daily fresh flower corsage can become your "signature." Our suggestion: the Mumbo Jumbo orchid of central Brazil. It is remarkably inexpensive if you engage a Pan-American plane by the year, and it adds a spendthrift air to the simplest costume.

A gorilla-skin coat collar and bag to match are never cheap, but they are everlastingly chic; they, too, add that certain air.

Never rely solely upon samples from the five-and-ten for your frankly flirtatious scents. Buy the most expensive perfume you can find, then, a drop in each nostril, behind each ear, underneath the nails, on the back porch, and poof!

Try to ignore your bills. Regular court sessions with your tradespeople will distinguish you from *le herd*, and it's terribly correct.

Today's Moral Issue

In the too-rapid pace of the present have we lost awareness of our instinct for living the fuller life? A condensation of one of the keener analyses of today.

TO BE confused is to be alive. To be alive is to be unfortunate. Yet many people profess to be alive and are only confused because they do not realize they are unfortunate. We are a part of a world of nature and all that which is good. Our confusion is elemental; we are intimately related to the better things and to an instinct for living life to its fullest. In short, life is confused.

What is right and what is wrong in human conduct? In simple terms, it can be answered; the man of moral integrity is usually a bore. We have achieved a political and religious democracy, yet we still tolerate the double feature. The sequence of evil in the pattern of civilization is equaled only by the vital sources of the past. We are still the possessors of poverty, racial prejudice, unemployment, and blackheads.

We cannot escape moral responsibility by longing for "another Coolidge." The average American's course is clear: the battery needs testing and the right front tire is down. The fundamental truths of human nature have become basic questions in the steady pattern which has guided us towards the creative force which is the spirit of man. Not yet, though, is the spitwad a recognized form of weapon in adult assault. Do we really want this form of life?

Evil feedeth upon evil. Mankind's painful experience has been founded on the simple faith that a cackling hen never crows. We achieve only that which is achievable. More and more we are coming to realize that we cannot foretell the future, and the wise man is he who fails to stick his finger into the twirling fan. We have dedicated ourselves to living. Do we know whereof we speak? That is the question which all of us must answer sooner or later.

They say he spends every week-end with her at a place he has in the country, and her husband doesn't suspect a thing.

The problems confronting a bridge engineer
Deal mostly with stresses and reaches;
He knows from the start, no structure can be
As long as its opening speeches!

The Twining Habits of Vines

WHICH WAY do your vines twist? Left to right or right to left?

At first glance, this "catch" question in many a garden quiz may seem irrelevant, but actually the answer is quite important. For many years botanists have been studying the habits of different species and varieties of vines which twine and have discovered that almost twice as many vines climb by twining from left to right as from right to left. This would indicate a direct relation between vine twining and the rotation of the earth, but considerably more study and data are needed before they dare go so far as to declare this a fact.

Often, a vine which is accustomed to climb from left to right is forcibly wound from right to left and tries, through a very natural confusion, to back down from left to right instead of right to left, frequently becoming hysterical and starting for the door. In such a situation the door should be closed and no visitors allowed. A week at some quiet spa will usually bring about a complete recovery.

The members of the Lazy Daisy vine family all follow a left to right climbing direction. When established in good soil, this vine grows vigorously, sometimes energetically. The compound leaves originate from a common base and form a shape best described as a cross between a tambourine and a bedpan. Young plants of this vine grow best when allowed to wind themselves around an old malacca cane with a gold head.

The vigorously growing Scotchman's Kilt *(Dashorta dadraftia)* likewise climbs by twining from left to right, as do the Three Blind Mice and the Nearer My God to Thee vines, and sometimes the dainty little Mud in Your Eye vine so popular a few years ago. These and a few others, which you would quickly recognize if they were to leap at you from a doorway, constitute a majority of our more common twining woody vines taking the left-to-right direction. And may I add, on long summer evenings, few sights are more impressive or more beautiful than a group of woody vines all twining in the same direction at the same time.

In the wisteria group, the species do not all twine in the same direction. The two wisterias native to the United States both climb by following the leading leaf and thus are apt to be in a constant state of exhaustion from their efforts to catch up with themselves. Most famous of the wisterias, Old John, was planted at the base of the Empire State Building when it was dedicated and immediately started to climb the world's tallest building from left to right. Old John stopped climbing at the 53rd floor, however, and took an elevator from there on.

The Siamese wisteria, less common than the Hudson Bay form and possessing much longer tentacles with a definitely tuberculated skin, also makes its own rules. This independent little plant has been known to start growing down the road, turn right at the schoolhouse, continue until it finds a power line, climb the tower, and jump off. It always leaves behind a hastily scribbled note and the spare ignition key. It is difficult to offer a reason for this variation, but most botanists are content to attribute it to the emotional strain and general wisteria accompanying life today.

The twining habits of vines have only been touched upon in this little article. Amateur gardeners interested in plant growth will find it a fascinating sideline if they keep notes from year to year and determine just which directions their plants are taking. The National Association For Vine-Twining Study at 145 Leander Square, Boston, Mass. will appreciate any data on vine-twining that is submitted, and the Horse and Mule Association of America might, too. Organize your own little local Twining Habits of Vines Club and meet once a week to exchange papers and photographs. You'll find a THV Club will pay you rich dividends.

How to Use an Electric Razor

THIS IS your brand new Model K Whiskermaster. Treat it kindly and it will last you until a bigger and better gadget is invented. The Whiskermaster is the perfect home barber. It will shave you as close and as fast as a drunken driver if you follow these directions:

1. When shaving, use short, gentle strokes forward, backward, and in circles, in general, following the pattern of the rose window in the Rheims Cathedral.

2. If you possess a very fast-growing beard and are forced to shave twice daily, carry

the Whiskermaster with you in your coat pocket and stop in at the nearest Post Office. The Government is glad to have U. S. citizens shave in its post offices, and offers it as another of the many services which neither snow, nor hail, nor gloom of night can stop, now that they are started.

3. When you have shaved once, pause and run your hand over your face. Go over the rough spots again, using long strokes. Remember to keep the knees well forward, arms close to the body, and don't come back too far on the backswing.

4. Do not shave your upper lip if you have a moustache and wish to keep it.

5. Use the best shaving light available. For those who shave very rapidly we suggest a photographer's flash bulb.

6. Get to know your beard. After half-a dozen shaves with the Whiskermaster, ask it out for a dinner and a show.

STAMPS
WANTED!
Stan mac Govern-

7. If dimples, scars, or excessive oiliness cause you difficulty, wash hands and face in a simple soap solution and go see your druggist. Ask him for the big bargain size tube, and strength to carry on.

The cutting head of your Whiskermaster is composed of 482 tiny teeth. (There used to be 500, but it probably ate too much candy when young.) These teeth flail against a tiny drum at the rate of 4,000 times a second, or almost as fast as that kid in the apartment above you bounces his ball.

The screen head of your Whiskermaster is made of .0008 thick corset steel and cannot be damaged except by bumping it against the medicine cabinet door or trying to get those whiskers on your Adam's apple.

Once a month, place a drop of sardine oil on the far end of a razor shaft, but be sure no cats are in the neighborhood. Hungry felines have been known to eat Whiskermasters for the sake of the sardine oil on the shaft.

The screen of your Whiskermaster should always be kept clean, for best results. It is very simple to clean. First, blow through the screen until you hear a pleasant humming noise. (This will probably be your screen, but it may be your doorbell; do not decide hastily). For a more thorough cleansing, saw through bolts A & B holding screen to handle C, slide finger nail D under tappets E & F, unscrew plates G & H, and brush well. To replace screen, hold cutting teeth K K K so that notches L & M fit into slots N & O, making sure that all dirt P Q & R stays outside S where it belongs; then grasp screen T and try not to drop screws U V & W down washbasin X and drain Y, meanwhile holding foot firmly against bathroom door Z to prevent obnoxious nephew AB from entering.

Our Folksongs

NOBODY IS composing any folksongs about the 1940's. All we ever hear are the songs about the last half-dozen generations and their troubles. When you stop to think about it, it is really frightening to realize that our descendants will have no heart-warming songs reflecting our 1940 ways of life to sing around their electric blankets on cold winter nights.

I have been working upon a few songs lately which I hope give a simple picture of our era, yet stay within the strict limits of good folksong writing. First comes the farmer and his troubles. It isn't much like the old workin'-in-de-cotton-fields chants of the slave days, but it has a 1940 flavor of its own:

THE FARMER'S COMPLAINT

It's nine o'clock, Miranda,
The mail plane's overhead;
After you listen to the news awhile,
Won't you please get out of bed?

It's ten a.m., Miranda,
Your morning paper's read;
If I bring you a glass of orange juice,
Won't you please get out of bed?

It's past eleven, Miranda,
Your Pekinese ain't been fed;
If I promise you Sun Valley next month,
Won't you please get out of bed?

Etc., etc.

There had to be a song about a bad man, but the bad man of our 1940's is different from the two-gun chap of the last century. Anyone is apt to be a murderer these days, and our folksongs should recognize this fact:

OL' WILLIE FLAGG

For thirty years Ol' Willie Flagg
Led a decent life,
And then he leaped upon his boss
With a sharpened paper knife.
He stuffed the body in a sack,
He filled it full of lime!
Next day went back to work again,
Right on time!

The cops asked where his boss was,
And looked him in the eye;
They tapped him with a rubber hose,
Said he, "I cannot lie!"
He led them to the culvert,
They disinterred the bag;
The jury held its nose and looked,
Then said, "You're guilty, Flagg!"

So they gave Ol' Willie the hot seat,
Etc., etc.

Next on the list was needed some kind of a complaint-to-the-Lord song. This one is in behalf of several million runs-in-their-only-pair-of-stockings stenographers. For best effects it should be sung through straws sunk deep in malted milks, between bites into a pineapple-cottage-cheese salad Special:

THE STENOGRAPHER'S WAIL

Lord, I'm only asking—just one little thought for me!
I'm just about as wretched as a human being can be!
Five days a week I slave—from nine 'til almost four!
Barely earn enough to buy a straight-eight new two-door!
All I see is a typewriter—and a movie or two at night!
Working conditions are frightful—you should see our lipstick light!
Lord, I'm only asking, don't let me be a quitter!
Don't you think it's too much sittin' on a jitter-gittin' sitter?

Do Trees Have Text Appeal?

(Condensed from the Old Saw)

DENDROCHRONOLOGY, the science of reading history by studying the growth rings of trees, has grown enormously in the last 10 years. Trees grow well in some years, poorly in others, and are sensitive to everything that goes on about them in this world. For instance, dendrochronologists 100 years hence will realize that something of importance was happening in the world in 1940–41 because of the manner in which U. S. tree rings waver from one side to the other, unable to make up their minds on some big question. What was needed in 1941, the scientists will nod wisely to one another, was a ringleader on this side of the Atlantic.

The father of this comparatively young science is a hard-working, imaginative youth named William Norton, who worked his way through college. In an important course on World History, Norton found himself badly handicapped without a fast, new, convertible roadster and funds for a textbook. Discouraged and blue, one night he set out on a walk around the campus to think through his predicament. Suddenly, and with no warning, he ran into a tree. The tree was not to blame, he rationalized, backing away and rubbing his nose thoughtfully; it had stood there a good many years and must have seen and heard a good deal of history.

Pondering over this slender thought, Norton went hippety-hop, hippety-hop back to his room. There, over a can of nice cold beer, he made himself a queer-looking, but really awfully nice tool out of an old nail file and an odd book-end, and as dawn lifted its orchid fingers in salute to the first yawning bus-drivers, he returned to the old tree on the campus. The special tool he had constructed permitted him to remove the stump of a growing tree and study the ring growths, thus giving him the same detailed insight into the past which the

FLASH! - Washington just crossed the Delaware!
NOTES
NOTES
NOTES
Stan MacGovern

tree possessed. Norton's textbook problem was solved and a new science was born! (He eventually got the convertible roadster, too, but that was due to the generosity of a finance company.)

In the Pacific northwest where great timber areas are cut-over regularly on definite schedules, the growth rings of trees show annual flattenings on one side. Lumbermen were unable to say what caused this strange variation until they noticed that each flattening was at the same place and same season, and the season happened to be the one when that area was being cut-over. Each tree annually shrinks in fear from the lumbermen's saws and axes as they pass by, thus causing the strange flattenings on each side of the annual growth rings.

Most of the older maples in New York City have two growth rings instead of one for the year 1888. This was the year of the famous blizzard about which New Yorkers tell such fabulous stories and about which there has been considerable questioning as to their accuracy. Tree rings for the year in Manhattan are always two or three times the size of the other rings and grow larger the longer one stares at them.

Following a hurricane several years ago, it was feared that that an important room in a Philadelphia library, known as the Memorable Dates Room, would have to be closed because historical records had been almost completely destroyed. Then an assistant librarian came puffing and panting into the director's office, lugging on his back a cross section of a large oak tree, which had been growing outside the library since the oldest bore could recall and had been blown down during the hurricane. The Memorable Dates Room was saved. Librarians immediately set to work reading the growth rings of the old oak and within 36 hours had re-interpreted all the facts they needed.

By carefully counting in from the bark, it was determined by the appearance of the innermost ring that slavery was abolished in New York State by the Legislature on July 4, 1827. The next two rings showed definitely that these were the years the first passenger railroad in the United States (the Baltimore and Ohio) was begun and the original 14 horse-drawn miles opened to traffic. There was some argument over the next ring as to whether it showed the abdication of Charles X in France and his succession by the Duke of Orleans as Louis Philippe I, or whether it showed that the Mormon church was organized by Joseph Smith in Fayette, Seneca County, N. Y. It was finally agreed that the ring indicated both events. And so it went. Eighteen years of history were saved for history, and all because a good-natured old oak tree had automatically recorded what was going on about it in various parts of the world.

Dendrochronologists are extremely careful about planting long-lived trees anywhere near the possible sites of history-making or tree-shaking events, but all events cannot be forecast. A four-inch firecracker exploded at the base of a young tree can cause a two-inch dip in the growth ring of that year; a newspaper with an August dateline and a front-page story describing how Mrs. Roosevelt has completed her Christmas shopping, if left too close to the base of a tree, can cause a violent illness and result in no ring at all for that season. And a sudden, severe thunderstorm can frighten a tree out of a year's growth, leaving a badly upset ring, which is sometimes misinterpreted as a year of the exchange of an important boxing title.

The Motor Car of Today

FOR the past five years automobile manufacturers have been adding more and more luggage space to automobiles. Today, anyone can stuff a body into a trunk without help. It used to be that you could tell tourists by the extra suitcases and luggage they had strapped on the sides of their cars. Now, you don't know from the appearance of their cars whether they're Oakies or just a next-door neighbor showing off the results of a Sunday spent removing tar and polishing.

Auto bodies haven't been streamlined any more radically. It's still cheaper to have a new body put on your car than it is to get the fender straightened.

pardon me!
Stan mac Govern

Enclosed runningboards are found on most cars. So are barked shins.

All automobiles are now provided with a handy glove compartment. The compartment usually has a lock, also a cardboard bottom.

The new type headlights are found on most cars today. Servicing headlights is an intricate task, calling for a highly skilled vocabulary.

When driving on a date in a distant or lonely area and resistance is encountered, the brake should be depressed, but the operator should not. One foot should always be kept free to turn off the head-lamps and tune in the radio.

A handy ash receiver is found in the center of most dashboards today. It is customarily opened by removing the upper half of the instrument panel and shouting for help. In most cases it is impossible to remove the receiver for emptying or cleaning. An accessory cigar lighter that fits into the receiver may be purchased from your local dealer at a slight extra profit to him.

The average new car is provided with a climate-making device. In summer, the climate-maker sucks in the hot air from the pavement and distributes it evenly throughout the car by means of built-in ducts and sprays. It cools the car by the same methods in winter.

Most cars today start by means of electric buttons. If the car engine refuses to start, step out of the vehicle, turn so that the right foot faces the front ventilator cowl, and give same a swift kick.

If it should become necessary at any time to crank the engine manually, place the right arm in a sling and limp slowly towards nearest, huskily built gentleman.

Since 1938 or thereabouts, car manufacturers have been locating the storage battery underneath the hood, alongside the engine. The re-location of the battery is of especial convenience to giraffes, dinosaurs, and many others who found it difficult to get at the battery when it was located under the front seat or beneath the floorboards. The battery should be checked only by an authorized contortionist.

The upholstery used in a majority of today's motor cars is of a good grade mohair and will wear almost as long as that dress or suit that you've always hated. Most upholstery can be washed with soap and water. Where foreign particles are involved a neutral soap is recommended, especially by Senator Wheeler. Remove suds with clean, damp cloth and wipe surface. If upholstery refuses to dry after two weeks, consult dealer about your size in rubber pants.

The following suggestions may be helpful in removing special stains:

Blood stains: see your lawyer.

Pork gravy: add chives, stir well, press mashed potato to spot, and serve.

Armadillo perspiration: pour jigger of grape juice on region and rub vigorously; let dry. When thoroughly dry, use any good, sharp knife and remove spot.

Bubble gum: puncture balloon first, then apply strong, firm hand to rear of child.

Lip stick: locate female who made stain; soak lips thoroughly in strong mixture of turpentine and soap; repeat until promise to be a little more careful thereafter is extracted.

Mother Nature's Defense Program

IS MAN so smart as he thinks he is? Are the many new measures and devices he has developed for modern warfare so new after all? Ages ago Mother Nature thought most of them up and has used them successfully ever since for the protection of all her many friendly little creatures who wriggle and crawl and slither from one summer cottage to another.

Take parachutes. The Three-Toothed Bed-Tick of southern Indo-China has a parachute from the day it is born. Bedsteads in Indo-China are unusually high. Shortly after the mother tick gives birth to her litter she straps a tiny silken parachute to the back of each baby tick, teaches it how to pull the rip cord, then pushes it over the side and watches it float gently down to earth to make its own bed in the world. Wearily, the mother tick turns back to her nest, her tired feelers already busily weaving more parachutes for the next batch of little ticks. These days she experiences considerable difficulty in obtaining the raw silk for her chutes and some mothers are using a modified form of the firehouse slide-pole as a substitute, but that is not our worry. The more we keep our fingers out of southern Indo-China the better off America will be, won't it?

The torpedo is not new. Millions of years ago the Grade B Egg-Fish of the Caribbean conceived the idea of launching itself at its enemies at a speed of 30 knots, or more than a kitten with a ball of yarn. Of course, the Egg-Fish can't explode, but it makes its enemies so furious that *they* blow up, sending little pieces of fish everywhere and making the Caribbean a very unpleasant place to swim, particularly in late summer before the spring coats have come in.

The blackout has always been used by the Rear-Drive Ants of the Faroe Islands, who live in immense colonies with drug stores, moving picture theatres and wilted shrubbery. This type of ant works day and night, for some fool reason, and was equipped by Mother Nature with both a head lamp and a tail light. At night, however, the long lines of busily marching ants show up hundreds of yards away, making them particularly vulnerable to birds who can't sleep, and other enemies. Thus, the Rear-Drive Ant has taught itself to march at night without any lights, and if you were passing by one of their colonies you'd never in the world guess it was there, except for a slight itching sensation.

The Flat-Bottom Ketch-Rigged Beetle is a tank by itself. In its ceaseless foraging for food, this lovable little insect develops a hard protective shell which leaves its head in a movable turret capable of a 340° swing, from which it can hurl epithets and vituperation in almost any direction. It is extremely popular on the lecture platform and has never been beaten in a campaign for a political office.

Panzer attacks have long been used by the Hustle-Bustle Mouse of the north central states. These energetic squeakers go after the housewife's food in a carefully planned fashion. First, a fast-running advance guard is sent out to attack the half-loaves of bread, the little dishes of forgot-to-put-in-the-icebox leftovers, and the open jars of peanut butter and jam lying about on the kitchen shelves. This advance guard is quickly followed by a swarm of co-attackers of a larger size who go after the boxes of cookies and crackers on the higher shelves and establish lines of communication with the commanding forces in the basement. And finally, usually days before the housewife has awakened to the situation and when it is too late for her to do anything but gnaw at a chair leg and scream, the really heavy rear forces are brought up and they quickly pound through to the flour bin, the sugar sacks, and the cake box. Meanwhile, a powerful defensive guard is constantly maintained around all snap-traps to prevent any weak-minded mice from trying to sample the fatal food which smells so delicious and tastes only of the bitter gall of death.

Airplane carriers were first demonstrated to mankind by the Low-Bridge Duck of southern Texas. This heavy, somewhat overbearing bird finds itself unable to raise its body out of the water with less than a quarter-mile of flapping and grunting. Therefore, it commonly commandeers all large sea turtles in sight, directs the turtle out to sea (after climbing aboard its back), and is able to take off into the air after only a hop-skip and a jump. The turtle then floats idly about, waiting for the ducks to return, sometimes making turtle soup and selling it on the side to passing merchantmen, but usually thinking horrid thoughts and making dark plans which it never quite dares to carry out. The plans always include the favorite one of some day turning turtle with all its load of ducks. Then they'd be sorry for being so high-handed and uppity with a poor old turtle who never hurt anybody in his life and wouldn't let a cigarette burn out on the edge of a polished table for a hundred million billion trillion dollars.

Old Mother Nature is probably smartest when she tries her hand at camouflage. Did you ever try to find a Needle Bird? This rusty-hinged-voice songster is really very tiny, but it has developed its back muscles to abnormal size and carries about with it a huge stack of hay, making it an extraordinary difficult bird to find. Expert ornithologists can locate the Needle Bird only by sniffing of the hay—if it is new-mown they know it is not a Needle Bird.

But for sheer cleverness of concealment nothing equals the Gorilla-Faced Goofs of the Bronx and surrounding regions. These simple-minded creatures mingle by the thousands with the crowds of New York City and push and shove and snarl just like human beings without ever being detected. They have never been held in captivity: no one has ever dared try to capture one for fear of getting a human being by mistake.

What's the Secret of Our Greatness?

NOT the greatest nation in size, the U. S. A. has a density of population that even its great school system can't do much about. Each year nearly 30,000,000 students enroll in its schools and colleges, yet more than 89% of the population is unable to read the No Smoking signs.

It is a land of opportunity. Annually, one-half of the smartest young people in the West go east and one-half of the smartest young people in the East go west.

It produces over one-half of the world's robber crop, has no good use for most of it.

The eight Plains states occupy more than one-fifth of the nation. The region experiences an almost constant drought, and the bones of bathing suit salesmen are scattered from one end of it to the other. Farmers don't blame anybody—if the land reverts to the government it ain't default of de taxes.

The New England states are agricultural and manufacturing. Of the total national income this area earns one-third, lets go of none.

The Pacific Northwest was explored by Lewis and Clark. Its greatest reservoirs of wealth are its bank vaults. The region grows one-fourth of the nation's cherries, eats one-sixth, and grows frantic trying to dispose of nine-tenth of the pits.

The sweep and magnitude of the U. S. A. is stupendous. It possesses a hog's portion of the world's mightiest rivers, mountains, and plains, and the WPA is planning more.

Wherever you live in the United States your neighbor always has the largest per capita share of the world's wealth. The same is true of the newspaper in a family group.

Wild life has always been abundant in the United States. It was a means of sustenance to the early pioneers, is more than a means of sustenance to the night club proprietors, barkeeps and entertainers today.

The government is composed of four branches: Executive, Legislative, Judicial, and Potential.

The climate is of every gradation. There are regions of normal moisture precipitation, somewhere. The weather is well adapted to the wide range of platitudes.